Original title:
The House of Comfort

Copyright © 2025 Creative Arts Management OÜ
All rights reserved.

Author: Tobias Winslow
ISBN HARDBACK: 978-1-80587-074-6
ISBN PAPERBACK: 978-1-80587-544-4

Symphony of Stillness

In a chair that squeaks with glee,
I sip my tea, feeling free.
The cat on my lap, what a sight,
A furry ball napping, pure delight.

The clock on the wall ticks so slow,
Each tick is a drum in this show.
The goldfish thinks he's a shark,
In water so still, it's a lark.

The fridge hums a tune in the night,
When leftovers dance in pale moonlight.
The couch is a throne for lazing kings,
Where laughter and snoring are the best of things.

So here I reside in blissful peace,
With quirky moments that never cease.
In this giggling realm, we thrive,
Creating joy, we're hilariously alive!

Always in Bloom

In a garden where the socks grow,
And all the plants wear hats, you know,
Daisies giggle, tulips dance,
While squirrels throw a daring glance.

Bees in shades of neon buzz,
Discussing life like little fuzz,
In this patch where laughter soars,
We chat with veggies about outdoor chores.

Lullabies of Love

Crickets play their nighttime song,
While pillows join the sleep parade along,
Teddy bears with sleepy eyes,
Share secrets in the moonlit skies.

Snuggles warm like fresh baked pie,
As pillows bounce and giggle high,
In dreams where jellybeans abound,
And everyone wears slippers upside down.

Radiance in Repose

In pajamas bright as a sunflower's glow,
We lounge like champions, just taking it slow,
Chips in hand, we laugh and munch,
While remote controls take the front-row punch.

Naps are scheduled, or so we say,
While books are read in a quirky way,
Elephants in tutus softly prance,
As laundry piles engage in a dance.

Memories in Motion

With each squeaky step, there's a story to tell,
Of pizza parties and candy to sell,
Nutsy adventures, cartoonish scenes,
In our playful land of quirky machines.

Tickles and giggles in every room,
Where dust bunnies swirl like confetti in bloom,
We toast to the chaos of each silly feat,
Chasing laughter, life's truest treat.

Corners of Kindness and Care

In corners where laughter spills wide,
Old chairs with tales, friends by our side.
A cat on the couch, snoozing away,
    Dreams of tuna, in soft sun's ray.

Warm cookies drift through the air,
Their scent like a hug, beyond compare.
The mismatched socks, a quirky sight,
    Each pair a laugh, a joy outright.

Embraced by Familiarity.

The fridge hums a soft, silly tune,
While forks and spoons dance in the afternoon.
Neighbors pop by with goofy grins,
Trading bad jokes, where humor begins.

The clock ticks slow, time plays its game,
In pajamas stained with coffee's name.
Laughter echoes off the painted walls,
As comfy slippers complete the calls.

Whispers of Warmth

Mismatched mugs, sipping tales of glee,
Where tea parties flourish between you and me.
The plants nod, eavesdrop on each word,
In this gentle haven, laughter's not blurred.

Cozy blankets pile up to the sky,
While silly stories make the time fly.
A tickle fight erupting from nowhere,
In the warmth of our joy, who would dare?

Nook of Solace

A nook stuffed full with moments and cheer,
Where boredom's banished, we hold it dear.
The old game box, a treasure so bold,
Unleashes giggles, and memories unfold.

The potted plant with a crooked grin,
Winks at the chaos, it's a win-win.
As storms may rage outside our door,
Inside, we laugh and find so much more.

A Glint of Light

In the corner, a lamp does dance,
With a bulb that flickers, given the chance.
We trip on the cat, who thinks he's sly,
While the pizza delivery guy walks on by.

The fridge hums a tune, a melodic beast,
As we gather for snacks, our nightly feast.
Dancing in shadows, we laugh and we tease,
Life in this chaos, a joy to appease.

Threads of Affection

Socks mismatched, a fashion faux pas,
But we strut our stuff with a cheer and a jaw.
The couch is our throne, filled high with old crumbs,
As we plot our stories of giggles and drums.

A blanket fort rises, a castle of dreams,
Where we hide from the chores, crafting our schemes.
With laughter as glue, our friendship is stitched,
In threads of delight, no moment is ditched.

Nestled in Nostalgia

Photos hang crooked, memories dear,
Each tells a tale that brings back good cheer.
The dust bunnies waltz, a scandalous sight,
With the vacuum in waiting, prepared for the fight.

Grandpa's old chair, it creaks like a boast,
As we swap mischievous stories, we're totally engrossed.
With coffee cups clinking, the night takes its course,
In this ship of fond moments, we're anchored with force.

Sway of Safety

Under the eaves, the raindrops report,
The weather outside can't steal our rapport.
We're wrapped in our laughter, a cozy cocoon,
Making trouble together, like a classic cartoon.

The world can be wild, like a circus in flight,
But in our snug nest, everything's right.
With pillows as shields, we brace for the storm,
Here, in our laughter, we've created our norm.

Melodies of Memory

In a kitchen where spoons dance around,
Pots and pans make the silliest sound.
A cat on the counter, aloof and proud,
Chasing the shadows, feeling quite loud.

Grandma hums tunes with rhythm and cheer,
While the dog joins in, adding a sneer.
Together they form a mischievous band,
With laughter and chaos that's simply unplanned.

Rays of Reassurance

The couch is a cloud, inviting and grand,
With cushions that giggle at each gentle hand.
A remote that's lost, hiding in plain sight,
Turns movie nights into silly quests, what a delight!

Sipping sweet tea while the ceiling fan spins,
As the cat takes a dive into a pile of sins.
Every nook has a laugh, every cranny a story,
In this lighthearted realm, we bask in glory.

Soft Places to Fall

A bed that's a trampoline, bouncing with zest,
Pillow fights break out, who's winning? The best!
Fortresses built out of sheets and old dreams,
In this realm of laughter, nothing's as it seems.

The rug's a safe harbor for wayward feet,
As socks disappear, they're never discreet.
Landing in laughter, we roll and we play,
Softness surrounds us, keeping woes at bay.

Whispers of Home

Echoes of giggles rush through the halls,
Where silly old portraits just observe it all.
A sneaky raccoon in the pantry at night,
Turns leftovers into a comical fright.

The doorbell rings, delivering glee,
With friends bringing snacks, oh what a spree!
In corners where whispers hold secrets untold,
The heart of our laughter is purest of gold.

Longing for Light

I search for a bulb that's not burnt out,
In shadows where dust bunnies flit about.
The couch has become a vast ocean deep,
Where snacks are aplenty, and napping's a leap.

Yet every creak feels like a haunted song,
Is it the house? Or did I just eat wrong?
The window's cracked, where the sun likes to peek,
Bringing cheer, but the cat ruins my week.

Haven's Embrace

Amidst muffin crumbs strewn near the chair,
I find my solace in half-done repair.
The couch is a nest of misplaced old socks,
Each pile a reminder of all my bocks.

In corners, dust gathers like friends after years,
Each cobweb a tale shared over cold beers.
I giggle as cushions go flying all day,
Who knew my refuge would play such a play?

Guardian of the Heart

The fridge hums tunes like it's a nightclub,
Each snack a dancer, each soda a dub.
The laundry piles up like a mountain of dread,
But oh what a comfort, my cozy bedspread!

Here laughter echoes, like a cat in delight,
As I slip on mismatched shoes, what a sight!
Every corner a memory, or fabric of dreams,
This quirky abode, bursting at the seams.

Rooms of Reverie

Whispers of ghosts in the creaky wood floors,
Tell tales of clumsiness, love, and wild chores.
The curtains are dancing, with no wind in sight,
Could it be spirits, or just an empire of light?

When the toaster explodes like a fun little bomb,
Breakfast becomes my ideal sitcom.
Here every misstep is a reason to cheer,
In this funny big fortress, there's nothing to fear.

Embrace of Familiarity

In my pajamas all day, what a sight,
Spilling coffee, it feels just right.
The cat on my lap, a true throne,
Ruling my kingdom, all on its own.

Snacks in the pantry, chips piled high,
With every crunch, my spirits fly.
Friends drop by, they won't knock,
They know my door's just a wooden block.

Sanctuary of Shimmering Shadows

Here the sunlight dances on the wall,
Casting silly shapes—oh, look at them all!
Dust bunnies twirl in a comical swirl,
A ballet of chaos in a lazy whirl.

Old chairs creak like they're telling tales,
Of all the laughter and funny fails.
The clock ticks loudly like a metronome,
Timing my day in this comfy dome.

Hearthside Echoes

With the fire crackling, I read aloud,
A mystery novel in a snug crowd.
The sofa's a ship, sailing on dreams,
Each pillow's a wave bursting at the seams.

In the corner, the plant's looking spry,
Can it really chat? Giving it a try!
Echoes of laughter fill the air,
As socks go missing, unaware, beware!

Refuge of Respite

Cushions piled up like a mountain high,
Diving in feels like soaring sky.
Lunch on the couch, who needs a plate?
Spaghetti jumper? No time to wait!

A blanket fort with a secret door,
Adventure awaits just a leap and a score.
My dog's the king of this fluffy land,
Together we rule, side by side, hand in hand.

Pillows of Peace

Fluffy clouds that catch your dreams,
A battle cry of snores it seems.
In a fort made of sheets and glee,
Napping heroes roam carefree.

Cupcake crumbs on every sleigh,
Snack attack before the fray.
With every pillow-packing fight,
Nap time wins, and all is right.

Corner of Contentment

A chair with snacks that rule the day,
Socks mismatched in an artful way.
Cat curls up to join the spree,
While sitcom laughs set spirits free.

With a blanket draped in pockets wide,
I'm buried deep, like I've tried to hide.
Remote in hand, I'll start the show,
And eat like it's a circus, don't you know?

Tranquil Retreat

A bubble bath with rubber ducks,
Scented steam and very few yucks.
A book awaits with tales of cheer,
As laughter echoes, bright and clear.

Duckling floats and bathrobe sways,
'Till I forgot the laundry's ways.
A splash, a squeal, oh what a scene,
In my oasis, I'm the queen!

Warmth of Woven Memories

Grandma's quilt is a cozy maze,
Wrapped in hugs from yesterdays.
I spill hot cocoa, it's quite a feat,
But laugh it off, it's still a treat.

Family stories twirl and tease,
As I dodge my cousin's sneeze.
We share our dreams between the seams,
In this warmth, we chase our dreams.

Sanctuary of Softness

In cushions deep, we dive and roll,
A fortress built for every soul.
With snacks galore and laughter loud,
Our silly antics make us proud.

A blanket fort beneath the stairs,
A kingdom where we share our cares.
The cat's a knight, the dog a dear,
In this soft realm, there's naught to fear.

With every giggle, joy expands,
Like pudding cups in sticky hands.
So grab a snack, let worries cease,
In our soft space, we find our peace.

Whims of Welcome

The door swings wide, a wacky grin,
As mismatched socks and chaos spin.
We welcome all, both near and far,
With laughter that's as bright as stars.

From silly hats to quirky shoes,
Some can't decide which one to choose.
With tea that spills and cookies tossed,
We claim the chaos, not the lost.

Come join the fun, we dance and joke,
With every word, a little poke.
In these odd halls, you're never late,
For fun awaits, no need to wait.

A Nest of Memories

In every corner, tales abound,
Of silly falls and leaps unbound.
We craft our stories, thread by thread,
In this warm nest, no need for dread.

From board games played till late at night,
To battles won with sheer delight.
With every laugh, a moment bright,
Our hearts are full, our futures light.

We build a world where blunders reign,
With cupcake crumbs and soda stains.
Each funny slip, a cherished grace,
In our dear nest, there's always space.

Comforting Cadence

With beats of life, we sway and spin,
Here, every smile's a goofy win.
In mismatched rhythms, we find our beat,
Where clumsy steps make life so sweet.

The kitchen hums a quirky tune,
As pots and pans join in at noon.
We twirl around like dancing fools,
In this wild groove, we break the rules.

Laughter bubbles, the joy won't end,
With every note, we find a friend.
In this strange dance, our hearts collide,
With silly songs, we swell with pride.

Foundations of Tenderness

In the kitchen, cookies lie,
Flour fights, oh my, oh my!
Spatulas dance, a funny scene,
While the cat steals the jellybean.

Socks on the floor, what a view,
A laundry pile that's just too new.
Bouncing pillows, a soft retreat,
Where laughter makes the days complete.

Couches claim their rightful space,
A remote found in a weird place.
TV on, the snacks they fly,
As silly films make time zoom by.

Surprises wrapped in old newsprint,
Leftovers dressed in a sweet hint.
Yet beneath it all, a joy so keen,
In messy lives, love is seen.

Embraced in Light

Sunshine spills across the floor,
That old dog snores, what a roar!
Chasing shadows, a playful game,
As the kids shout, 'Let's do it again!'

Lampshades wobbly, shining bright,
One flickers, gives a little fright.
A dance with dust, oh what a play,
While the toaster thinks it's a café.

Amidst the chaos, voices blend,
Silly stories that never end.
Each giggle shared, a spark ignites,
Wrapping us all in warm delights.

Beneath the roof, our quirks align,
With tangled cords and cups of wine.
In every corner, laughter soars,
In this light, our hearts restore.

A Melody of Moments

Morning chatter fills the air,
Pancake flops, none seem to care.
Syrup rivers on breakfast plates,
As the dog snags toast, oh, what fates!

Outside, the garden's all a mess,
Weed wrestlers in a floral dress.
Bumbles float, and giggles grow,
While the neighbor's cat puts on a show.

In the living room, dance we must,
Tickling toes, laughter a must.
Record player spins a laugh,
As the kids work on their autograph.

And as the clock ticks on its way,
Another tale, another play.
In this song of joyful cheer,
Each note reflects, "I hold you dear."

Portraits of Peace

On the wall, a family tree,
With silly faces, all for free.
Each snapshot shares a different grin,
As memories dance, let the fun begin.

The fridge is full of doodled notes,
A fish with legs, and silly quotes.
While leftovers hum a tune so sweet,
In every bite, the joy repeats.

Outside, the swing set sways and creaks,
As laughter rings, the moment peaks.
A parade of socks, mismatched charm,
Creating a memory, safe from harm.

So here's to the quirks we hold dear,
In these portraits, we adhere.
With every smile, and joke retold,
We find our love and warmth unfold.

Echoes of Laughter and Tears

In a room where socks are mismatched,
And the cat plays chess with the dog,
There's a legend of spilled hot tea,
As giggles unleash from the smog.

The fridge hums a tune of despair,
While a pizza lies under the bed,
Together we dance, two left feet,
As chaos reigns in our head.

A plant on the shelf sways along,
To the rhythm of laughter and cheer,
With cushions that double as pillows,
We cradle our worries in here.

So raise your glass of fizzy pop,
To all the silly times we've shared,
In this mess of a life we adore,
Where every moment has been bared.

A Cuddle of Clouds

On a couch made of crumbs and dreams,
Where daydreams float in a pile,
The ceiling fans twirl like sassy dancers,
As we munch on snacks with a smile.

Our dog wears a tie, quite dapper,
While the cat steals my slice of pie,
Laughter erupts from stuffed animal friends,
As they join in our joyful high five.

When rain drums a beat on the roof,
We play games that make no real sense,
A choir of squeaky toys in the chorus,
Singing songs of fervent pretense.

In this cuddly abode of delight,
Where pillows become our close kin,
We find joy in the simplest moments,
Where the fun never seems to thin.

Cradle of Forgotten Melodies

In a corner where old tunes lay still,
And dust bunnies dance to the past,
We uncover the song of our youth,
While giggling and hoping it lasts.

The record player skips on a whim,
As we join in a chaotically tune,
With socks on our hands like old mittens,
And we sing to the glow of the moon.

A ukulele joined by wild laughter,
Plays notes that are slightly off-key,
Yet harmony blossoms in each blunder,
As we relish in moments so free.

So strap on a smile and let's play,
In this cradle of silliness sought,
For every melody shared in our mess,
Makes each echo a treasure well caught.

Abode of Kindred Spirits

In this nook of quirky oddities,
Where mismatched chairs tell a tale,
We spin yarns of spatulas and socks,
As giggles punctuate our trail.

The chandelier sways like it's dancing,
With polka dots and a tiny crown,
We wear our hearts like mismatched shoes,
As we laugh the frowns upside down.

The wallpaper whispers sweet secrets,
Of mishaps and tales of delight,
As we sip on that questionable brew,
And pretend that it's all quite alright.

Here's to the silliness we share,
In our sanctuary of pure cheer,
May the echoes of joy linger longer,
In this place where we conquer fear.

Sheltered Serenity

In a place where socks do roam,
And cereal's a forgotten home,
Each cushion tells a funny tale,
Of snacks and naps that never fail.

Walls adorned with mismatched art,
A cat that thinks he's really smart,
We laugh at dust bunnies on the run,
In this cozy spot, we have our fun.

Chairs that squeak like old folk's knees,
Piling up with crumbs and cheese,
A blanket fort is where we thrive,
In silly smiles, we feel alive.

Here, chaos reigns but hearts are light,
In pajamas from day to night,
Where laughter echoes, broad and loud,
We find our joy, our quirky crowd.

Nest of Nurture

Cushions gather like a warm hug,
While dishes pile like a sad rug,
At this nest, laughter is key,
Who knew spilled juice could taste so free?

Spider plants dance in the breeze,
While socks go missing, if you please.
Each corner holds a joke in wait,
A world where none can feel too late.

Tea stains on the perfect chair,
Complaints of crumbs floating in the air,
Every laugh spills over like tea,
In this cluttered place, we feel glee.

Amidst the chaos, bonds grow tight,
Sharing giggles, morning to night,
In our nest, where quirks expand,
A refuge built by silly hand.

Refuge in Radiance

Lights that flicker, shadows play,
With mismatched socks on full display,
We dance around the untidy floor,
While the dog greets you with a snore.

Mugs of cocoa with marshmallow caps,
Forty-seven blankets for cozy naps,
Coffee stains like abstract art,
In this warm glow, we find our heart.

Giggles echo as the door swings wide,
Friends tumble in, prepared to collide,
In this refuge, we crash and cheer,
Where even the odd seems oddly dear.

Through all the mess, a light shines bright,
Filling up our souls with delight,
Here's to moments, imperfectly spun,
Laughing together, each day is fun.

Cradle of Calm

Sweaters piled like a fuzzy hill,
Where time is ours, we pause and chill,
Laughter flows like a gentle stream,
In cozy corners, we live the dream.

A toaster pop, then crumbs that fly,
As friends devour the leftover pie,
Here, every mess is simply styled,
In our arms, the world feels mild.

Puddles of giggles, unspoken grace,
Our quirks embrace this favored place,
In this cradle, worries take flight,
With every toast, we toast to light.

Calm wrapped in chaos, our perfect blend,
Where every heart can truly mend,
In laughter's grip, we rise and fall,
Creating joy in our little hall.

Sanctuary of Solitude

In a room where socks play hide and seek,
Worn-out chairs talk secrets, oh so bleak.
A fridge full of leftovers, a feast of despair,
The cat conspirators plotting fresh air.

Dust bunnies dance to a tune of their own,
While coffee spills like a royal throne.
TV reruns paint the walls with glee,
Welcome to my kingdom, where I'm king bee!

Loud silence echoes in each dusty cranny,
The remote control's my best friend, uncanny.
Cushions embrace like old friends in need,
A fortress of laziness, that's my creed!

So raise a toast with a slice of stale bread,
Where the joys of being home are often widespread.
In this quirky retreat, I roam and roam,
For nothing feels better than my comfy dome!

Dappled Light of Leisure

Sunbeams wiggle through cracks in the door,
While I snooze on the couch, dreaming of more.
A cup of tea spills, not a worry in sight,
Oh, the perils of dappled daytime delight!

Pajamas my armor, they fit just right,
I'm a couch potato and it feels so bright.
Projects abandoned in the corner heap,
With snacks on my lap, I settle to sleep.

The clock ticks slowly, mocking my stay,
Who needs adventure on a sunny day?
In the hammock, I swing, lost on a whim,
Every moment at home makes my spirits brim!

With books piled high like a towering cake,
I ponder the dangers of hitting the lake.
But what's that? The fridge calls my name with a cheer,
I'll just grab some leftovers and stay right here!

Places Where Time Pauses

In my den of delay, I take my throne,
Where the clock seems confused, forgotten, alone.
With slippers that squeak like old grandpas,
I lounge in my fortress, ignoring all laws.

The dishes stack high, a small Mount Everest,
But who wants to clean? I'm truly not stressed.
The dry plants salute me, proud and intact,
They know in this lair, there's a sacred pact.

The fridge hums a tune, a musical friend,
I tap my toes lightly, it's a dance that won't end.
Books and old blankets, a fort I have built,
Each laugh echoes softly, free from the guilt.

So here I shall stay, in my pajama-clad hide,
To explore every crumb that my cookie jar hides.
In this whimsical place where minutes don't flee,
Time's made an arrangement to sit here with me!

Elysian Echoes

In the corners of chaos, laughter unfolds,
Where slippers attack, and each sneeze is bold.
Whiskers waggle as the door swings wide,
An endless parade of snacks on the side.

Walls whisper secrets of coffee wars fought,
Between spilled chocolate and pudding that's caught.
The echo of giggles bounces off beams,
As I lounge like a king in the land of my dreams.

Pillow fights reign as the pets watch with flair,
With popcorn avalanches raining despair!
Yet every mishap heightens the thrill,
My comfort kingdom thrives, it's my greatest skill.

So let the world swirl outside in a rush,
I'll roll in my blankets, no need to hush.
For here in this space, with a grin I declare,
Life's best moments bloom where we don't have a care!

Little Luxuries of Life

A sock that's warm, not full of holes,
A fridge that hums, and never trolls.
Soft bedsheets that make me feel like a king,
A pizza delivery—that's the real thing.

The remote that's found, just under the couch,
A laugh that erupts, not a single scrouch.
Sweet snacks galore, hiding in plain sight,
Bubble baths bubbling, oh what a delight!

Chirping birds sing their morning brew,
A comfy chair with a stunning view.
Socks like clouds, cozy and bright,
Little luxuries that feel just right.

Dreaming in Daylight

Sunbeams dance on my windowpane,
As I plot my nap, in my brain.
A blanket fortress, my fortress bold,
Dreaming of tacos, and never cold.

The cat takes my spot, oh what a tease,
While I'm dreaming of hammocks and mild breeze.
The clock ticks slow, it's a fishy plot,
Time sure can drag while trying to snooze a lot.

A sandwich made with leftover pride,
Is just the fuel for this sleep ride.
Dreams sprinkle joy, light as a kite,
In my sunny haven, oh what a sight!

Graced with Gratitude

Thanks for mismatched socks, oh what a trend,
For every spilled snack, it's a laugh, my friend.
Each spoon that clinks against the bowl,
A reminder to cherish this goofy role.

Gratitude for plants that don't need a green thumb,
And snacks piled high; oh, the joy's never numb.
The coffee that brews with a comforting hiss,
Every sip a hug, it's pure bliss!

For friendships that bloom like a quirky bouquet,
And silly moments that brighten the gray.
In laughter's embrace, we find our way,
Graced with gratitude, every day!

Quiet Corners of Calm

The nook by the window, where silence hums,
A cushiony treasure, it softly becomes.
A cup of hot cocoa, with marshmallows piled,
The world fades away, just like a child.

The old cat snores, a lullaby true,
While I ponder life, and the things to pursue.
A good book awaits in my sunlit domain,
With characters quirky, they too are insane!

Here lie the worries, as light as a feather,
In quiet corners, we feel light as weather.
Peace hugs my soul, in this nook of mine,
Finding calm joy, like sipping fine wine.

Cloistered Charm

In a nook with socks that don't match,
The cat's found a throne on the scratch.
Gran's cookies whisper, calling my name,
While the plants have taken up the blame.

The TV blares, but no one's awake,
The dog snored so loud, it shook the cake.
My cousin's hair is a wild, gold mess,
Yet we laugh at him more, we must confess.

Jigsaw puzzles lie in disarray,
Last seen in April, footprints of clay.
Why can't we clean? A mystery to all,
But who needs dust? We've got this ball!

We dance like no one cares to see,
In mismatched clothes, feeling quite free.
This funny chaos, so dear and bright,
Wraps us all in its odd delight.

Embraced by Familiar Walls

The walls lean in, they like my jokes,
Hovering over me are family folks.
They serve up stories, some true, some not,
You laugh till you cry—forget what you sought.

Crumbs line the couch like a cheesy trail,
Popcorn fights prove we shall not fail.
A game of charades? My sock puppet's deft,
Wins 'fore the snacks are forever left.

The fridge hums tunes of the vast unknown,
Mysterious leftovers, past their throne.
Yet every bite brings a smile and cheer,
Each taste a memory, each sip a beer.

At the table, jokes are flying high,
Still holding our sides while we've got pie.
In a circus of love, this place spins my heart,
With giggles and warmth, it's a work of art.

Enclosed by Love

Where slippers roam and laughter spills,
Beneath the roof, the time stands still.
The phone rings loud, it's Auntie's prank,
As we fix her hat with a silly yank.

Cousins wrestle like they're in a ring,
The dog's become part of their fling.
With every tumble, we erupt in glee,
This chaos, our dance, forever free.

Cupcakes decorate the dinner plate,
While Dad's lost the recipe, that's just fate.
We blame the cat for the floury mess,
Say it brought the fun, yes, I must confess.

Under rugs lie secrets, socks galore,
With each little slip, we tumble for more.
Together we create a beautiful storm,
In this quirky place, we always feel warm.

Heartfelt Haven

With mismatched chairs and a creaky floor,
This refuge pulls me, forevermore.
A sofa that swallows me whole, it seems,
Where laughter and love mix like sweet dreams.

The coffee cups dance like they're alive,
Each spoon's a partner, oh how they jive.
We spill stories like tea, warm and bright,
In this cozy den, all feels just right.

Socks peek out from behind a chair,
They argue about who's got flair.
While Mom ponders where her glasses went,
The cat just smiles; it's a perfect event.

Under the roof with no real plan,
We're a clan of quirks, the best kind of jam.
Together we giggle, in this funny fight,
In our haven of warmth, we'll always unite.

Symbols of Serenity

In my comfy chair, I sit and snooze,
Dreaming of tacos, wearing my shoes.
Socks inside sandals, a fashion delight,
Juggling my snacks while I binge on a bite.

My cat rules the roost, with a purr so loud,
While I try to eat, she's drawing a crowd.
Napkin on my lap, it's a food-fight affair,
Who knew that spaghetti would fly through the air?

The bubbles in the bath, they dance and play,
Soap must be laughing, it rolls away.
Floating like rubber ducks in a race,
Splashing the walls, now that's my happy place.

Evening rolls in, with pizza on the way,
Mouth watering, I sing, it's a glorious day!
Friends gather round, they're all such a treat,
Spreading the joy, with laughter we eat.

Oceans of Openness

In my backyard pool, I float like a whale,
Sunshine above, holding a frosty ale.
Swimmer's tan lines marking my domain,
Splashing like dolphins, causing a stain.

The garden gnome watches, his smile is sly,
As I belly flop in, almost reaching the sky.
My neighbor's green grass is perfect for lawn,
But my cannonball makes it look like a pawn.

Children nearby screech, in pure delight,
While I do the backstroke, it's a hilarious sight.
Mom on the sidelines says, "What a mess!"
Yet my floaty's a crown, I feel like the best.

Evening draws near, with fireside cheer,
Roasting marshmallows, oh give me a beer!
Crickets provide their evening chorus, too,
This life's a big laugh, I'm telling you true.

Porch of Pleasantries

On the porch swing, I sway to and fro,
With lemonade dreams and the sun's golden glow.
The neighbor's dog barks at nothing I see,
I giggle and think, he must be barking at me.

Chairs squeak beneath while I kick up my feet,
Talking to birds, they seem pretty sweet.
A squirrel steals peanuts I left on the rail,
Chasing it off, I unleash the loud wail.

Faded old cushions, with patterns so bright,
Holding my snacks in the warm summer light.
The radio plays tunes from way back in time,
As I dance alone, it feels so sublime.

Suddenly a breeze shakes the leaves on the tree,
Whispers of secrets between you and me.
Here on my porch, lunacy feels like fate,
Where laughter and joy are never too late.

Everlasting Embrace

In the comfort zone, where socks unite,
Wearing my pajamas, oh what a sight.
Sprawled on the couch with snacks piled high,
It's a cozy gala, come give it a try!

The warmth of the blanket, bewitching my soul,
We're watching old films, it's out of control.
Cringing and laughing at each silly scene,
In every embrace, there's a joy that's serene.

Calls from old pals, they echo with cheer,
Texting on the sofa, oh not so severe!
Chiming in laughter, like rings on a phone,
This friendship is vintage, it's finely grown.

As the night darkens, with popcorn we cheer,
For the joy in our hearts, we hold pretty near.
In this goofy realm, with laughter as grace,
Every silly moment's an everlasting embrace.

Aromas of Affection

In the kitchen, smells of stew,
Garlic dances, onions too.
Cakes that rise, muffins that fall,
Who needs a gym when there's food for all?

Baking cookies, flour in my hair,
'This is a style!' I boldly declare.
Chocolate chips; better than gold,
Sweet little nuggets, never get old.

Friends gather 'round, laughter fills the air,
Whisking up tales of old, with humor to spare.
Burnt toast? A treat we can barter,
It's blackened, yes, but it's still a starter!

So pass the pie, and share the cheer,
Even the mess brings joy, I fear.
With every bite, so many smiles,
In this kitchen, love multiplies.

Stillness in the Heart

In my chair, I sink and sigh,
The clock ticks loud, as the minutes fly.
A cozy blanket, a sip of tea,
Who knew peace could be so cheesy?

The cat purrs softly, a furry fountain,
Dreaming of mice on a fluffy mountain.
I join in dreams, like a sloth on a spree,
Wondering how I became one with the sea.

Outside, the world is a noisy song,
But in this nook, it just feels wrong.
I chuckle at chaos, I sip, I bask,
Finding calm is my favorite task.

So here's to stillness, let's raise a toast,
To lazy days we adore the most.
For in the quiet, space to play,
It's my kind of wild, in the mellow sway.

Bowls of Kindness

In my kitchen, bowls stack high,
Filled with sprinkles that shimmer and fly.
What's that? A soup from last week's spree?
Nope, just a puzzle – where's the key?

Spaghetti spills like a happy dance,
Tomato sauce, a saucy romance.
With noodles entwined, we feast and laugh,
Who knew carbs could write a whole paragraph?

Salads tossed with humor and glee,
"Is it a side or a main?" yelled me.
A bit of this and a sprinkle of that,
Creating chaos like a cat in a hat!

So join the feast, let humor delight,
In every bite, laughter takes flight.
Bowls of kindness, garnished with cheer,
Come eat with us, we've plenty to share!

Havens of Hearth

In my humble home, chaos reigns supreme,
Dust bunnies host their very own dream.
Cushions askew and toys on display,
Who needs order on a Friday playday?

A rug that once was bright, now a tad gray,
Whispers secrets of wild kids at play.
Under the couch, I find a whole snack,
Pizza slice? No, just a mystery pack!

The walls echo laughter, and sometimes a shout,
As my dog joins in, ready to pout.
With warmth in the oven and joy in the air,
This crazy little space is beyond compare.

So here's to the mess, the fun, and the noise,
Embracing the mayhem with love and poise.
For in these havens where whimsy starts,
We'll cherish our lives, with full, happy hearts.

Embers of Connection

In the kitchen, a dance ensues,
Spaghetti flinging like party shoes.
The dog steals a meatball, what a sight,
Laughter erupts in the warm evening light.

Grandma's knitting is fondly admired,
But the yarn becomes what the cat desired.
Threads all tangled, her patience thin,
We laugh as we lose, what a silly win!

The couch is a fortress, pillows on guard,
Each seat a battle, no room for the charred.
Remote control wars, who gets to choose?
The innocent bickering is never a ruse.

Yet in these moments of playful jest,
We find our strength, we find our best.
Through laughter and joy, we hold it tight,
Our embers glow softly, through day and night.

Doorways to Dreams Unfolding

Knock-knock jokes echo through the hall,
Behind every door, there's laughter's call.
The closet a portal to worlds so grand,
Where capes make you fly, let dreams expand.

A pillow fort's walls, a treasure so dear,
Where whispers of secrets fill with cheer.
Bedtime tales turn monsters to munchies,
As giggles replace all the evening crunchies.

The bathroom becomes a stage for a show,
With toothbrushes dancing, stealing the glow.
Soap bubbles rise, like popcorn in air,
Our sparking delight for all to share.

Together we weave a tapestry bright,
Of dreams that take flight in the soft nightlight.
With each playful door opened wide,
We find little treasures where giggles abide.

Shelters of the Heart

In this refuge, socks do not match,
But who cares when your dreams are to hatch?
The couch holds secrets of comfort and fun,
With springs that creak like a dance on the run.

The fridge is a canvas with leftovers grand,
Magical meals crafted by eager hands.
Pickles and ice cream find unity rare,
Who knew that a snack could bring so much flair?

Stray kittens and lawn chairs form a parade,
Where silly ideas are boldly displayed.
The yard becomes home to unwelcome quests,
Like searching for treasures in the old garden's nests.

With silly traditions that make us all laugh,
Each quirky detail adds to our craft.
In this cherished space, where hearts never part,
We build funny stories, our shelter, our heart.

Oasis of the Everyday

In cups of coffee, spilled dreams we sip,
While curtains flutter like a magic trip.
Granola spills like confetti on the floor,
Every crumb a reminder to giggle and soar.

The clock ticks loudly, a dragon's roar,
Yet time turns silly, and we laugh even more.
Chasing after moments that slip through our hands,
We turn mundane into whimsical bands.

On rainy days, we jump in the puddles,
With squeals of joy that muffle our cuddles.
The washing machine sings a rhythm divine,
While socks conspire to lose the straight line.

In this delightful, chaotic ballet,
We find our oasis in the silliest play.
For life is a canvas, brush strokes of glee,
In our everyday world, we paint brilliantly free.

Sanctuary of Solace

In a chair that squeaks and groans,
The cat claims all the comfy zones,
With snacks piled high on every shelf,
I chatter to myself, just like an elf.

The TV plays the same old show,
I laugh at jokes I already know,
The fridge hums sweet serenades,
As I stir my coffee with a handful of blades.

My slippers and I, quite a pair,
We journey nowhere without a care,
The curtains dance in a playful breeze,
Life's greatest challenge? Finding the keys.

So here's to naps and silly plans,
Building castles made of cans,
In this quirky nook, I'll stay and dwell,
It's a riot, my friends, but I won't tell!

Embrace of Familiar Shadows

In corners lurk my dusty books,
And sock-puppets with questionable looks,
The plants nod kindly, though they dread,
The truth that I might forget to water them, instead.

The fridge light flickers like a disco ball,
As I dance around eating leftovers, oh how they call,
Chasing crumbs like a detective keen,
In my world of chaos, I'm the queen.

My coffee spills, like life's own jest,
Draped on the couch in my comfy nest,
Friends come by to join the tease,
We'll laugh till our sides hurt, if you please.

So here's to shadows that offer a grin,
And the giggles that always begin,
In every haunt, a story's spun,
Who knew solitude could be this fun?

Hearth of Whispering Dreams

A blanket fort, my royal throne,
With snacks and stories, I'm never alone,
I host wild feasts for imaginary friends,
While my dog concedes, "This madness never ends!"

The oven beeps a tune so sweet,
As I pretend my baking's a magical feat,
Flour flies as I swirl and spin,
If the smoke alarm sings, let the chaos begin!

Each night brings a quest, a start anew,
With pillows as armor and dreams as my crew,
In this realm where giggles are king,
I reign supreme, the jester and the bling.

So gather round for tales untold,
Where laughter's currency makes you bold,
In this enchanted space of silly schemes,
We find our bliss in whispered dreams.

Refuge Beneath the Roof

Under this roof, peculiar sights,
Adventure brews on lazy nights,
With mismatched socks and grumpy glares,
The dog sprawls, boundless in his lairs.

The clock ticks loud, a mockery clear,
As I ponder life over last night's beer,
The blankets heap like mountain peaks,
With popcorn storms when I dare to sneak.

A comedy show, just me and my thoughts,
As I practice my jokes and tie up my knots,
The mirror laughs back, a mischievous glance,
As I show off my best silly dance.

So here's to quirks and the laughter they bring,
As I embrace the joy of everything,
In this haven, where chaos and fun meld,
I'm the king—at least until the pizza's held!

Nest of Gentle Echoes

In corners where dust bunnies play,
The cat naps, dreaming of fish fillet.
Cushions shout, 'We can hold you tight!'
While chairs conspire to start a pillow fight.

The fridge hums tunes like a pop star's blare,
It keeps leftovers with love and care.
Each teapot whistles a warming song,
As socks engage in a tugging throng.

Windows peek out, with curtains that sway,
Birds gossip gossiping in the ballet.
The broom does cha-cha while sweeping the floor,
Creating a rhythm to open the door.

A space so quirky, filled with delight,
Where laughter echoes and all feels right.
In every nook, a chuckle awaits,
In this lively nest, joy never abates.

Heartstrings and Homesteads

The kitchen's a chaos, a spoon on the run,
While pots and pans battle for who's number one.
The coffee pot fumes, brewing a tempest,
As toast does a dance, trying to impress.

In the hallway, shoes form a tangled parade,
They hold conversations, never afraid.
The vacuum hums gossiping tales from the floor,
Spilling secrets the dust bunnies swore.

A plant by the window appears to pout,
For every time it asks, we just move out.
The couch, like a magician, swallows the remote,
What did we watch? Who would even vote?

It's a circus of comfort, a delightful mess,
With heartstrings that play in a cheerful dress.
Here in our homestead, where oddities bloom,
Laughter and love fill every room.

Pillars of Peace

In the living room, a giant TV roars,
While a cat claims the seat, pondering scores.
The coffee table's a fortress of snacks,
As cousins wage war with popcorn attacks.

The walls are adorned with scribbles and art,
Created by hands, bursting with heart.
Each picture misaligned, a beautiful crime,
Mocking perfection, one stroke at a time.

The sofa whispers, 'Just take a rest!',
While pillows declare they're the very best.
The clock chuckles, ticking at its own pace,
Sure it has all of the time to embrace.

In this wacky realm, laughter takes lead,
Each moment, a treasure, a genuine seed.
Pillars of peace in this home we create,
Where humor and warmth always celebrate.

Warmth Within the Walls

Here laughter dances down the hallway wide,
As quirky remarks on the sofa collide.
The fridge plays gossip, chilling tales of delight,
While the stove joins in for a sautéed fight.

In the den, mismatched socks form a team,
Competing in styles, a vibrant dream.
The curtains, with flair, flutter and boast,
About the grand parties they host the most.

A rug tells stories of spilled drinks and snacks,
It covers the tracks of mischievous acts.
The lights sometimes flicker, claiming a ghost,
But we laugh and assert they're the ones we toast.

So here's to the warmth within these walls,
Where quirky memories hang and call.
Joy is the fabric, stitched strong with a thread,
In this vibrant retreat, we're lovingly led.

Sighs of Serenity

In slippers worn and coffee spills,
We dance around the lunchtime thrills.
The cat rolls by, a furry mess,
While socks in corners play hide-and-seek, I guess.

The fridge hums loud a lullaby,
As leftovers join the food supply.
With laughter echoing off the walls,
And finding crumbs in all the stalls.

When friends drop by for snacks and cheer,
We joke about the missing pier.
The couch holds secrets, stories, and dreams,
And silly antics by the beams.

So here we sit with joy and spills,
In our cozy nook, we find our thrills.
With every joke and every cheer,
We craft a home where love draws near.

Tapestry of Togetherness

The rugs are lumpy, yet we stay,
With pillows fluffed in a quirky way.
Our laughter rings like silver chimes,
With puns galore and silly rhymes.

In the kitchen, chaos reigns supreme,
As we concoct our wildest dream.
Burnt toast and noodles, what a sight,
Yet somehow, it all feels just right.

With board games strewn upon the floor,
And friends who laugh till they can't anymore.
Our grand escapes with spice and flair,
In every corner, a chip of care.

So let's embrace this joyful mess,
In our tapestry, we find success.
For in these walls, our hearts align,
Embroidery of love, oh how it shines.

Hearthstone Harmonies

The fireplace crackles, sparks take flight,
As marshmallows roast into delight.
With stories shared and smiles wide,
Our hearts grow warm beside the tide.

The dog snoozes with a blissful sigh,
While children twirl and mother flies.
A symphony of joyous sounds,
In our haven, laughter abounds.

Biscotti crumbs on a paper plate,
As friends debate if it's too late.
To binge on shows with late-night snacks,
With playful jabs and friendly acts.

So we gather here, a merry throng,
In harmonies where we belong.
With jokes and jests that never cease,
In our own world, we find our peace.

Safe in Shadows

The lights are dim, but oh, what fun,
We laugh and scheme, our time has begun.
In cozy corners of faded light,
We spin our tales into the night.

The bookshelf creaks with every tale,
Of ghostly whispers, or a silly fail.
With flashlights beaming on faces bright,
We weave our stories in sheer delight.

The blankets piled, a fortress grand,
A hideaway where dreams expand.
As shadows dance in playful form,
We chase the lines of the norm.

So here we sit, a merry band,
In this warm, whimsical wonderland.
With grins and giggles, we're never alone,
In our nooks of joy, we've made our home.

Unraveled Threads of Serenity

In a chair that creaks and sighs,
I rest my head and close my eyes.
My faithful cat claims half the space,
With dreams of mice, she takes my place.

Dishes pile like a treacherous tower,
While I pretend to work by the hour.
TV murmurs sweet, silly songs,
"Just five more minutes!"—where time belongs.

Pizza boxes stack mountain-high,
I'll climb them all, and I'll fly!
Socks in the fridge? I can't recall,
Just sprinkle in laughs; those are the best of all.

My coffee cup runs dry too soon,
Like my hopes of cleaning 'til noon.
But in this chaos, joy I find,
In the mess, my heart's entwined.

A Veil of Soft Hues

Cushions whisper, soft and round,
In joyful colors, laughter's found.
My dog plays king on a throne of fluff,
"Don't move!" I plead; he's just too tough.

Walls are covered in odd photos galore,
Grandpa's wig? We laugh and implore.
Curtains wave like they must dance,
While the vacuum's humming, lost in a trance.

Spilled coffee stains and popcorn rain,
Each little mishap brings joy, not pain.
A sanctuary where socks go rogue,
They find new mates in every old vogue.

The odd squeak in the midnight air,
Is it a thought or a ghostly dare?
Laughter echoes through every nook,
This place, my joy, I gladly took.

Haven of Rest and Rebirth

A blanket fort made for kings and queens,
Hiding away from all the routines.
Fortified with snacks and a screen so bright,
A realm of giggles fills the night.

Neighbors wonder, is that laughter or cries?
Tentacles of popcorn reach for the skies.
Kids bounce like jelly, uncontainable glee,
As we all chant, "Just one more movie!"

Laundry launched like an Olympic sport,
"Are those mine?" I ask, while I transport.
From living room chaos to bedroom bliss,
I stumble, I trip—wait—was that my kiss?

Old board games lie under a dusted sheet,
Expecting a dust-off, aren't they sweet?
Laughter and snacks, what could be better?
In this space, no need for a letter!

Corner of Quiet Reflections

I sip my tea, pondering life,
While dodging that old, pesky strife.
A mirror reflects my latest hairstyle,
Like a bird's nest that went out for a while.

Pillow fights break the silent air,
Who knew comfort could be so rare?
With mismatched socks and a pirate hat,
Every room tells tales; oh, imagine that!

Dust bunnies can dance, everyone knows,
They pair with the cat—to the music, they pose.
An empty fridge, with space so wide,
I chuckle and shout, "What's dinner tonight, wide?"

So in this corner, I'll sit and observe,
A patchwork of joy, and oh, the reserve!
With laughter and warmth, my home is complete,
If quirks are the norm, then life is a treat.

Hearthbound Whispers

In cozy corners, socks do roam,
Beware the gnomes that call this home!
With cookies stashed beneath the chair,
And pillows flying through the air.

The cat has claimed the warmest spot,
While humans freeze, just like a lot.
The TV blinks with random shows,
As popcorn dances, joy it sows.

Loud laughter bounces off the walls,
As holiday shows bring goofy falls.
We've lost the plot but found the cheer,
At every meal, we toast with beer.

Beneath this roof, we find our fun,
Sharing snacks until we've run.
We promise tales will never cease,
In this warm nook, we find our peace.

Cloistered Between Dreams

In fluffy blankers, dreams take flight,
While monsters hide, not quite in sight.
Bedtime snacks, a feast we munch,
As whispers float above the crunch.

With unicorns that roam the night,
And fairies lurking, oh what a sight!
The clock's hands spin like a wild ride,
In this kingdom, we dream with pride.

Under pillows, giggles abound,
In the chaos, fun is found.
Each spooky story brings delight,
As shadows dance, it's quite the sight!

Morning yawns bring sleepy frowns,
But breakfast always lifts us 'round.
In this realm, we reign supreme,
Cloistered snug, within our dream.

Shadows of Solitude

In corners dark, the dust bunnies play,
While socks go rogue, they run away.
The fridge hums tunes of yesteryear,
And lonely spoons find love, not fear.

A creaky floor sings quiet tunes,
To unseen friends, 'neath hapless moons.
With mismatched cups on every shelf,
We toast the joys of being ourselves.

Behind closed doors, the chaos lies,
In laundry mountains, laughter sighs.
Oh solitude, you're quite the friend,
Though funny tales, you never lend.

Yet in this silence, comfort grows,
With echoing laughter, the heart bestows.
In every crack, we find our sound,
Together in shadows, joy is found.

Elysium of Ease

In lazy chairs, we stake our claim,
As naps feel like a glorious game.
Remote in hand, we press and pause,
With snacks aligned, applause gives cause.

The world outside can buzz and whir,
While we indulge, oh what a blur!
Fuzzy socks on every foot,
In this setting, our joy's a hoot.

With sunshine peeking through the blinds,
We laugh at how life unwinds.
The cat walks by, majestic strut,
While we sit back, a cozy rut.

In this realm of sweet delight,
Where every hour feels just right.
Elysium found in such a breeze,
Here's to comfort with so much ease!

Wrapped in Warmth

In socks that match, I strut about,
With chips in hand, I dance and shout.
The couch my throne, a feathery land,
Where snacks and naps go hand in hand.

A blanket fort, my secret space,
Where dust bunnies claim the race.
I wear my crown, a paper hat,
While the dog conspires, bold and fat.

The fridge hums tunes, a lively beat,
A treasure trove of tasty treats.
And when the pizza finally arrives,
We feast like kings, oh how we thrive!

Each pillow stacked, a soft delight,
In this chaos, everything feels right.
With laughter echoing, friends so dear,
Wrapped in warmth, we know no fear.

Beneath the Canopy of Care

Beneath the shade of quirks and laughs,
A jungle gym of silly gaffs.
The dog's a lion, the cat a bird,
In this realm, absurd is the word.

The plants are gossiping, I swear,
They talk of squirrels and the trees' bare hair.
Pajama days stretch out so wide,
We're adventurers on a couch ride.

Cookies bake, another batch,
Their sweet aroma, a perfect match.
With board games sprawled across the floor,
Each time we play, we laugh some more.

A quilt of joy, all tossed around,
In this cozy chaos, comfort's found.
With tickle fights and stories old,
Beneath this canopy, warmth unfolds.

Cradled by Kindness

In the land of snacks, we reign supreme,
With ice cream scoops, we dare to dream.
A pillow mountain, we climb so high,
Where giggles scatter, oh my, oh my!

The remote control, our magic wand,
We summon laughter, of which we're fond.
With every sitcom's wacky twist,
We bond and banter, and we can't resist.

The dog takes charge, our furry king,
His bark, it echoes, what joy it brings!
As we pile on, a cuddly heap,
With kindness sprinkling like fairy dust deep.

The world outside can spin and whirl,
But in here, we dance, we jump and twirl.
Cradled by friends, in warmth we shine,
In this silly haven, it's simply divine!

Safety in Stillness

In corners rich with sleepy sighs,
We gather here, 'neath lazy skies.
Each knitting needle clinks along,
While the cat hums a soothing song.

A cup of tea, the steam a dance,
While someone pranks, they take a chance.
With mismatched socks and wild hair,
Safety blooms in this quirky air.

Time ticks slow, no rush in sight,
We sip and laugh, all feels just right.
With pillows piled, a soft embrace,
In stillness, we find our favorite space.

Our secret stash of cozy dreams,
With belly laughs and silly themes.
In this realm, whatever the thrill,
We play and rest, in bliss we fill.

Tapestry of Togetherness

In the kitchen, we laugh and spill,
Pasta flying, what a thrill!
The cat, he's plotting his next great heist,
Swiping snacks, oh, how he's spiced!

Sock wars erupt on the living room floor,
With colors and patterns, who could ask for more?
Dad's on the couch, lost in a show,
While Mom's crafting chaos with glue and a bow.

Every corner has tales to share,
From cookie crumbs to the dog's wild stare.
We play charades, a scene gets crazy,
Grandma's dance makes everyone hazy.

The walls hold laughter, a radiant sound,
Echoes of giggles, joy unbound.
In this wild sanctuary, we thrive and roam,
Here's where we always feel most at home.

Serenity in Every Corner

Chill vibes float on a lazy afternoon,
Dad snoozes softly, like a big fat raccoon.
The dog dreams loudly, barking in sleep,
While Mom's coffee brews, oh, so deep.

That armchair's got tales of snacks and naps,
Full of crumbs and unexpected flaps.
A blanket fort built, a grand retreat,
Where warriors gather, bread crusts to eat.

Sunbeams dance on the cluttered floor,
As siblings plot, always wanting more.
Giggling softly, they hide and seek,
Whispers of secrets shared in a peak.

Every nook glows with memories bright,
From shoe prints to laughter, it feels just right.
In this realm of chaos, we find our way,
Trading silly stories at the end of the day.

Walls that Whisper History

These walls hold whispers, tales of the past,
From pranks that were pulled to food eaten fast.
The echoes of laughter are stuck in the paint,
While the dog plots revenge that is far from quaint.

Crayon drawings adorn the worn-down frames,
With stick figures and crowns, oh, such silly names!
A dent in the wall from a long-ago spill,
Reminds us of moments that gave us a thrill.

The attic's a treasure of odd, dusty things,
From hats to old photos with peculiar rings.
We rummage for fun, a quest to behold,
Finding mysteries wrapped in the old and the bold.

With every tick-tock, the memories dance,
Time's playful winks give us all a chance.
In this whimsical chaos, we gather and feast,
Creating new stories, the laughter's released.

Synthesis of Starlight and Shadows

Evening descends, the shadows grow long,
With pillow fights breaking out like a song.
The glow of the moon pours in through the blinds,
As our laughter echoes, no trouble finds.

The popcorn's a mountain, we're ready to share,
With movies and giggles, no worries to bear.
A furnace of warmth, we huddle so tight,
Crafting silly stories, until the good night.

In between pillows, our dreams intertwine,
As whispers of silliness make the stars shine.
Tickling the fancies of hearts big and small,
With bedtime antics that enchant us all.

Night wraps its arms 'round this cozy nook,
As we write tales within this storybook.
Stars wink above us, a celestial prize,
While joy fills our hearts, a wondrous surprise.

www.ingramcontent.com/pod-product-compliance
Lightning Source LLC
Chambersburg PA
CBHW060115230426
43661CB00003B/190